ARE YOU LOVING WHAT IS NOT LOVING YOU?

"Why do us women put so much time, emotion, energy into a man based on a hope. In return to only receive all that was given, a Hope."

DELADY

authorHOUSE®

AuthorHouse™ LLC
1663 Liberty Drive
Bloomington, IN 47403
www.authorhouse.com
Phone: 1-800-839-8640

© 2014 Delady. All rights reserved.

No part of this book may be reproduced, stored in a retrieval system, or
transmitted by any means without the written permission of the author.

This is a work of fiction. All of the characters, names, incidents, organizations, and dialogue
in this novel are either the products of the author's imagination or are used fictitiously.

Published by AuthorHouse   04/30/2014

ISBN: 978-1-4969-0887-2 (sc)
ISBN: 978-1-4969-0886-5 (e)

Library of Congress Control Number: 2014907872

Any people depicted in stock imagery provided by Thinkstock are models,
and such images are being used for illustrative purposes only.
Certain stock imagery © Thinkstock.

This book is printed on acid-free paper.

Because of the dynamic nature of the Internet, any web addresses or links contained in
this book may have changed since publication and may no longer be valid. The views
expressed in this work are solely those of the author and do not necessarily reflect the
views of the publisher, and the publisher hereby disclaims any responsibility for them.

CONTENTS

Emotions and Fear 1

Emotional Insecurities...5

Emotional Blindness 9

Uncontrollable Emotions...13

Emotional Anger...16

Emotional Disturbance 19

Emotional Success...22

Women, Men and Emotions.......................................25

Emotional Dangers 28

Woman That Emotional Machine 30

Love 36

Hugs and Kisses 37

Emotional Confusion 38

Exotic Lovers...39

Questionnaire 40

Conclusion 41

Acknowledgements

First and foremost, I would like to thank my Creator for a sane mind through all the sadness and madness in this world of trials. Next, I would like to thank my parents, my dad Kenneth Taylor (R.I.P.) for the little time we shared, and showing me how a man should see and recognized that I am special, needed, wanted and important. Thanks to mother, Orlyn Wormley for showing and giving unconditional love, which only a mother can. Then, I would like to thank my brothers Lamont, Duane, Mikeal and William for their brotherly love and for always being there for their only sister. My kids, Jazz, KK and Papa whom I will acknowledge by expressing my never ending love. I must also acknowledge my best friend Nicole Ross(girl we on to something Lol!)for being my best friend for many, many years. And last but not least, I would like to thank my man, friend, confidant, ears, shoulders, hugs, kisses, and most of all, for your wisdom of loving me that entails me to love you back.

Love Always,
Delady

Dear Reader,

The title is an ongoing reality between women and men from the time of Adam and Eve. Why is that a woman or women are always loving a man that does not love them back the way they wish to be loved? Before we begin to go deep within this volume of factional knowledge and experience. I must inform the reader, that this book will be controversial to some, enlighten to many, and straight to the point for those that truly understand the bio-physiological make-up of women and men. This book was written without assumptions, and furthermore without hypothesis, and also without great theoretical jargon. Last but not least, I must also inform the reader, that this book was written and put together by the author's personal experiences of growing up with her brothers, losing her father at very young age, and having a few relationships with men of normal status to ambitious business minded men. Women are producers of society, and men are looking at us women as though we are sexual machines! Something that produces many things that men in society utilizes for their personal gratification and survival needs. The core of all women is their emotional fuel, which is powerful, successful or destructive. Without women there wouldn't be a society, and it damn sure wouldn't be any great feelings or love as we know it. Women think with their hearts, they make decisions with their hearts, and they see the world through their hearts. The heart is the seat of emotions that functions totally on feelings. Men are rational-emotional beings, which entails them to be much more different when it comes to their emotional structure. Men are mental beings, and women are emotional beings. When it comes to women, majority of today's men assume they are the women's sexual operator to work them sexually in order to produce something. Whether it's a child, a form of mental security, finance, to make a home or obtain a job position. When it comes to men and women the relationship is a mental and emotional balancing act with great set-backs of twist and turns, which is nothing but the order of things that needs to be learned and considered. Women and men must work together to produce the fabric or item that comes from their joint production. This product they have created by their emotion and mental capacity represents their work in progress or decline. As we proceed further into this book, and you apply the wisdom and understanding presented to you, only then will you see your life, and relationship change with a great difference. This change will be greater than your sexual fantasy! This book will also leave your mind spellbound by the truth and realties that a woman has ever endured or imagined in her wildest dream to see intellectually and emotionally. All your misconceptions and doubts will be removed from your mind, and you will be presented with many ideas concerning new tactics, strategies and a unique relationship for a life-time. You will also see many things that you may have to strongly consider to change for yourself first and foremost, and then seek to change your present relationship. At times women have emotional battles with their hearts and minds. Their minds will torture them with many unproductive or productive emotional thoughts with great apprehension, that comes mainly from past personal relationships, and their physical make-up(*with all the weight-loss kicks*). Like a machine that produces, and endures much work overtime this machine begins to break-down and needs mechanical enhancements. So the body of women also changes due to age and its physical endurance over time. This plays a major part of women's emotions with great consideration, and massive emotional whirl-winds concerning their esteem and their role play in society. This society she helped create like her other women-sisters from ancient times to the present is her domain. There's an old cliché' that men have used for many millenniums when it comes to dealing with women, *"You can't live with them, and you can't live without them."* This can also go for women and men. Since, I have had my own personal experiences with men, knowing what they can do, will do, won't do, and what they're damn sure able to do. I wouldn't want to live without that one man, that has a winner's attitude with great masculine powers to achieve whatever he seeks to achieve. There's a saying among men that I heard once before *"One real lady will beat five funky tramps !!!"* Only if she's able to produce an ideal societal home-front first and foremost concerning her kids, the family, her man and herself. So lets proceed to understand and achieve, what is greatly needed to be understood, "(Why) Are You (Women) Loving What Is Not Loving You back!!!"

Author
Delady

Emotions and Fear

Before we dive into this great topic about emotions and fears, I would like to pose a question. Is emotion the cause of fear or is fear the cause of emotions? This question shouldn't have taken you long to answer. Emotion and fear are both a great sense of feeling. Emotion and fear are the same, which are feelings that tug and pull from deep within. There's a difference in their capacity for greatness or hindrance. A woman that fears losing a man that she truly loves can be a hindrance to her personal growth and the relationship. For example, let's say this man has a negative attitude, and his mental capacity is the mind of a loser and he is also abusive. Out of fear of losing him she'll remain with him due to her emotional bond. This example displays some serious things to acknowledge coming from any woman, that has been or that remains in this type of situation concerning her man. Now from this example, we see that some women are having the same serious emotional stressors and hindrance from a unhealthy relationship. Her emotions are tied, and wrapped up with fears that are causing her to remain in a relational dilemma that's hindering and filled with ignorance. Most women would say that, *"any woman that holds on to a man with a losing attitude and abusive behaviors only means she has the same losing attitude, or she must be stupid!"* That can be true, but we all have different concepts of what love is. The concept on how we see love, think about love, and what we feel about love determines the outcome of our relationships and future success. Women that didn't have a good father relationship compel them to grow up with a great psychological apprehension about men. It also causes the women to act and behave with insecurities. Some tend to look for a man that has an old man's demeanor, which resembles the father figure that she didn't have has a child. These insecurities are nothing but past failures, and a fear of being left alone again. So this leads her to act very uncouth and demanding at times. It has nothing to do with the man she chose to be with presently, unless he portrays the attitude of not caring about her feelings. This only brings back past experiences of being without a father or man in her life, when she needs or needed him the most. This only means a great cycle of being without a man, and emotional fear fueled with uncontrolled emotions. When it comes to women, no matter if that woman is a whore, a tramp, or a bitch she still have this impeccable desire to be loved deeply by a man. This great emotional endowment has been created by Father-Time and Mother-Nature, to have this great pull of electrical-magnetism that she gets from a man. The first woman she learns this feminine prose from is her mother, which represent unconditional-love and understanding, and she learns the masculinity from her father that represents strengthen, great mental prose, and protection. The mother and father bond helps to create a balance for the young-woman when she becomes an adult. So being without a male figure can be the reason why many of us women love what's not loving us. We are trying to hold this man by all means, because we have experienced what it's like to be man-less from our childhood. This puts an emotional strain on our mentality to not see there is more fruit(men) on the tree of society to pick or choose discreetly. Our great emotional psychology, which is surrounded or held down by fear, stops our intelligence from seeing the truth! That society still possesses some good men.

A woman has always been thought of as the one that keeps the family together, but this is only true when both fear and emotions are in their proper place within that woman. Emotions and fears can make the most intelligent, and well put together woman appear to be unstable. When emotions consume a woman majority of the time, all rational thinking is set aside or gone. Feelings of the heart will take over instantly, especially when dealing with those that are closest to them. Sometimes these emotions are further driven by fear. Fear may cause her to move in a way she may have never thought that she would act. That same fear could make her stay stationary. When emotions are high the energy in the body is high. With this emotional energy, women have been known to do some very silly, selfish and foolish things. That is why it is never good to make decisions when us women are very emotional. It's not good to make decisions when we are in fear of deciding. Emotions can make the fear greater, and fear can make emotions blind our intellectual capacity to make great rational decisions. Emotions have been known to wipe away all logic. What makes sense will no longer be an option, because now we are thinking with our heart and not with our brains. Regardless of how much emotions are deep within, we know that emotions will be in full affect guiding women to what women know or to that great unknown world. This world can be progressive or detrimental. It only depends on the decision made at that time. Whether the decision was rational without fear, or irrational with extreme feelings of pain or vengeance. This only sets the stage for vulnerability. Which in the long run is the push and pull syndrome by someone that uses this vulnerability for personal gains. Here comes the cycle of use and abuse. Only because women try to get over their emotional pain too quickly by jumping into another relationship without totally reevaluating themselves and their past relationships. So they look for someone to take their mind off their pain, which is emotion and fear that has taking over all rational thinking.

When it comes to emotion and fear concerning women and their kids, this emotional feeling has great power to protect, rationalize, and love unconditionally. Women can advise her daughter or daughters, and sometimes their son or sons on many things concerning her outlook and personal experience on how they(women) view men. (*Some women make great mistakes teachings their son(s), how to treat women. Women can only give their son the feminine emotional advise, which can be very detrimental because she's not a man. So how would she know how a man should treat a woman, if her relationships have been an emotional cyclone.*)This can be good or bad, it depends if the woman has an open mind to explain from her past experiences. Here's when emotion and fear for her children is for greatness. She wishes and hope that her daughter or daughters do not have the same bad experience with men that she had once before. So she provides rational advise with fear, hope, and emotional desire for greatness. Also, when it comes to the woman's livelihood with fear of being without economical assistance, and having dependents is very emotional to women. Her emotions will be that great fuel to do something to provide for her love ones. This love that women have for their husband, boyfriend, or their man, has many unseen encounters that has to be endured that will be put to the test sooner or later.

Majority of women don't like that word or thought of being put to the test, but they love the strategy that the men uses. This shows her that he has some intellectual intelligence. All women test men one way or another, but the word or thought of being tested slightly torments their emotional being. The test or emotional event will reveal great weaknesses or a powerful bond. This powerful bond must be respected and real for one another and from one another. One great hindrance that professional women encounter is when their relationship begins to breakdown when the success goes unchecked. Which means that the successful one begins to torment the other about lacking in the department for success.

This emotional breakdown can make the other one feel alone, cheated, disrespected, and fear of not knowing what to do. It also can make the other one feel compelled to do something. Usually this behavior comes from the men that are driven by emotional logic. This emotional logic is projected within the young men's psychology at a young age. These same young men will be driven by great emotions, with a logical twist to be successful at all cost. When he is striving for success, and it doesn't reflect what he's doing to achieve his success. This same man will lash out at his love partner (the woman), and blame her for not aiding in his personal achievement. Then his partner feels disrespected because she was there by his side when he didn't have anything. The woman's emotions will project many thoughts of doubt within her mind, and many feelings of apprehension within her heart. So in conclusion, emotion is a powerful tool that all humans possess for greatness or their own demise. So the bottom line of emotion and fear is they both are feelings that has to be approached with a rational mind by all means. Which can be detrimental or the fuel to achieve success. So without this fuel called emotion women wouldn't be women that produces the meaning of love. Love is emotion and nothing more or less!!!

EMOTIONAL INSECURITIES

There are many insecurities that encircle our lives 75% of the time, whether we're conscious or unconscious of it, it definitely exist. Insecurities play a major part in our lives, and it also leads us to make decisions from an emotional basis. Lacking confidence and strong self-esteem within ourselves, whether woman or man creates this emotional insecurity. When it comes to women there are many insecurities that confront and torment her has she becomes older. The children are growing up(if she has children), and living their own lives in a world of treachery and heartlessness. This triggers the love, and protection that the mother has for her children. This compels the mother to be overbearing, and prying into her child's life uncontrollably at times. She only does this out of deep love and concern. This deep love is a form of emotional insecurity that's wrapped up with great concern, that many mothers have no matter how successful her children may be. This force of emotional insecurity plays a major part of women's hopes, and wishes for her children's safety in a cruel world. Many mothers have learned how to channel this force of emotional insecurity. They ask and give advise from a caring perspective. Wise mothers know how to pry without seeming to be overbearing. At times this emotional energy can become overbearing, and causes some kids to believe their mother lacks confidence, and trust in their lives and decisions. This is only motherly love that the kids fail to understand until they have children of their own or they will grow to be wise enough with time to understand fully their mother's emotional concepts. This emotional mechanism that impacts women's emotional state forces them to put in emotional work for the children regardless of the time, place, people and actions to make a great difference.

One of the major things that afflict women concerning emotions other than her children or her child's future, is her present relationship. After having many or a few experiences with past relationships, emotions have the potential to inflict or jeopardize her present one. This emotional infliction comes from a detrimental relationship in the past. This emotional past tends to produce habitual unseen insecurities within a relationship that has the potential to be great or grand. Insecurities will put a great burden, hindrance, and emotional anger on the partner that's not insecure, but afflicted by his or her partner's insecurity. Not to go deep within the metaphysical or physics, when it comes to the logical standpoint of things physical, and the core of how nature works. The Law of Nature is the core of everything, when we have seen it from a logical stand point. Emotions can be very blinding to all things that's able to be seen rational, or logical when it comes to pain and disappointments from past experiences. The Law of Nature, is always moving which causes all things in this Universe to interact with one another. Whether the energy is negative to repel or positive to attract.

So being insecure causes the person that's insecure to act on that energy of thought. This thought will fruition depending on the magnitude of that emotional energy. That emotional energy that dwells within the heart of a woman, has the capacity to blow or breakdown similar to a machine.

Many men fail to understand why women carry this emotional warped physiological concept with them from one relationship to the next. It's because most men are the same, and fail to listen and ask the right questions concerning the woman's past. Not knowing where someone has been, and where they're coming from, you fail to know where they're headed and seek to go. If a woman left a relationship due to an abusive partner, and she jumps into another relationship with a man that's physically different, but acts abusive similar to the one she just left is due to her concept and internal judgment. This judgment comes from her self-esteem, and her wiliness to truly understand who and what makes her the person she is. Failing to know who we are causes men and women to make many more mistakes, when it comes to choosing a partner for life. Insecurities has more to do with the person that's insecure, more so than the person that causes or give reasons for someone to be insecure. One major mistake that all women seems to make young or old countless or numerous of times, is when the man or their boyfriend treats them intentionally wrong or bad. He willing apologizes to see if he can get away with it again. In other words he wants to see if the woman, young or old really likes him. So he puts her to this silly test, but that's his level of thinking. When she accepts his apology under the guise of his apologetic mannerism, so she falls for the setup, not knowing because of her emotional decision. She has just giving him the keys or the ok, for him to do more wrong. Since she let him get away with something wrong once, will only make room for it to happen again and again. Now she has created her own world of insecurity from the lack of understanding and accepting something she didn't like. This is only because she deeply feels and truly believe she is in love. Her emotional feeling of love allowed her partner the ability to use logic over her emotion for his personal gain.

Being in love whether young or old can be very detrimental. Young-men do not have the slightest idea what love is when it comes to a young-woman other than his personal family that are females. I have said this numerous of times, 'if a young-man truly loves and respect his mother, sister(s), and grand-mothers, he has the capacity to respect the young-woman, and grow to truly love her. Now, if she really loves and respects her father, brother(s) and grand-fathers with a close knit relation, she will not let any man use and abuse her by any means.' Some relationships are so content, that it breeds emotional boredom without emotional adrenaline or excitement that some women crave. Because of their past insecurities that fuels that fear of getting old, and losing their youth while growing old without someone can warp her emotional logic. Some women will accept abuse, lies, cheating, that has nothing to do with true love, but due to their emotional insecurity that's driven by emotional blindness, they will continue to stay in a unproductive relationship. We will expound on blindness and emotion as we move on deep within this book. We all have some insecurities whether lacking enough money, losing a job once before, losing someone we loved dearly in the past, and seeking to get married and it's not happening. I must say this, if you're a Blackman or Black-woman in America your greatest insecurity is the police and the courtroom. "Lol, Ha, ha!" Because of our present system of false liberty, false freedom, and racial inequality!

So I conclude, that emotional insecurities will always play a part of our lives that dwells deep within the man's psychological makeup, and deep within the woman's physiological make-up, which is an emotional roll-coaster.

Emotional Blindness

Let me pose a question. How can emotions be blinding, and how can emotions be seen? (*Many of us has close friends that are in a relationship that we fell are very unhealthy, abusive, unprogressive and manipulative.*) We all have said, "love is blinding!" That's only because we feel something that we have never felt before. Sometimes this feeling of love isn't love at all, until we claim it to be, then it is love from our understanding for it to be just that. No matter what someone close to us says concerning our unhealthy so-called love affair with this man, it's unheard and intentionally unacknowledged, due to the pain that will be endured when confronted. There has been times when a close friend has seen the other partner with another woman or man, and felt compelled to mention it to the other partner concerning that cheating partner's lies and screwing around(*which is none of our business*). We know even if we make mention of it, the other person will not believe it, because of her or his deep feeling of love for his or her partner. Coming from a bad relationship, who wants to hear some bad depressing news. The news might be true! Our emotions will not let us face that pain. Especially when we have all felt it before. It puts us in a state of vulnerability, and emotional disturbance that is equally painful to imagine or consume mentally. Taking these blinders off to see our partner's real self or just to see who we are can be just as fugitively emotional, than being told something concerning our mate.

Most men seek to have power and control over his woman at all cost. When he possesses this power and control he loses it by becoming very arrogant and machismo that feeds his ego. This ego puts man in state of emotional blindness, called ego. This ego makes man unable to see what his woman is doing, has done, and what she's attempting to do for them on a grand scale. Women are blinded by their heart, and man is blinded by his ego at times. Both species has to deal with emotions no matter from what degree, it does exist. What is blinding to one mentally, is also blinding to the other physiologically. This is when they should learn to complete the puzzle of life concerning their relationship. If the partner knows that the other is weak in a certain area, then that partner should be the strength that the other lacks. Once they have strengthen each other weaknesses or fill in the gaps that can make the relationship stronger; only then can they be able to face all types of adverseness. Most women that had a bad relationship, run to some form of so-call emotional security or means to prevent the harsh reality of emotional pain. Doing this only sets the stage for vulnerability, and she gives up her control to be ruled all over again. When a man comes to her rescue when she most needed it. She builds a strong friendship that grows, and this man becomes her means to confide in that appears to be that "prince and shining amour", that can be a toad underneath the gloss and shine. The more she depends on this man that came to relieve her from emotional distress-gives the man more power, control, and the means to do whatever he wants. Only because she will do whatever to hold him, and keep this emotional champion around by all means to dodge that great emotional pain. This emotional pain that she hates to face is nothing but emotional blindness, disguised and hidden emotional strengthen. This pain has been injected into her psychology from her past relationships, that she over looks herself, which is the real woman verses the artificial emotional hurtful woman. Another thing, I must make mention about men and their ego is their great desire for his mate and him to have a son. Majority of men today fail to greatly understand the 50/50 chance of a woman dying, the child dying or both of them dying during physical child labor. Three out of ten women die while giving birth to a child. Men fail to truly understand this great pain of labor that is very deadly. The mother's health and environment plays a great role to developing and shaping the child inside of her. These physical circumstances of the mother and child also depends on the body's chemical-balances. Men that pride themselves on having a son puff themselves up with pride about having a boy, but fail to be the man of great concern about the life and death encounter that his mate had endured.

When a woman is emotionally involved with a man, she's blind to the things around her. How she feels outweighs all logic. This emotional blindness will cause her to do what may otherwise never has been done. The world around her is nonexistence to her. All she sees is what her feelings have shown her. Most of the times this blindness is blown up, more so when a woman doesn't want to face what the truth may be. The people around her will see a total different story from what the emotionally blind woman sees. Everything that she does, and how she does it will be fueled by that blindness. This emotion can be fed by that someone the woman is emotionally blinded for greatly. What is obvious to others, maybe oblivious to the emotionally blinded woman. She is living in a dark fantasy world by her emotional blindness. This emotional blindness causes her to never make the right decisions at the wrong time.

This emotional blindness can cause her to never see what needs to be seen concerning her affair. Some women have come from a bad relationship, and can have a man that's totally different from her last, but she will carry those bad experiences with her without her noticing it. This causes her to be blindfolded to see a winner right before her eyes in the flesh. Some women seek to find a perfect man, which some women try like hell to find! This emotional blindness will force the woman to be very irrational, that she emotionally believes that a perfect man exists in this human fallible world. This form of thinking concerning a perfect man is not only irrational, but very delusional and ludicrous! Women that has been hurt once or many times before always says, "she wants a man that knows, or one that's good." One thing that I've notice about women that make comments like this, they are very indefinite with themselves. Which only means that she is greatly indecisive with her inner most self. Being indecisive causes her to make more wrong decisions and irrational actions.

Some women even lie to themselves, when they have kids by an abusive or cheating partner. They tell themselves they will remain with this man for the kids sake. The kids see and feel the pain, violence, abuse, and wish their mother, and themselves would leave this horrific detrimental situation. This deep love forces her to remain in a relationship that is based on lies and emotional blindness. Children that grow up in this type of environment usually portray these same behaviors in their own relationships when they become adults. Only because they have seen their parents act abusive to one another, that it seems right because their mother remained in this abusive environment. So this emotional blindness has been past down to her younger ones, only because of their mothers' emotional blindness, that's fueled by hope, low self-esteem and insecurities. So this emotional mechanism has to have the right operator to produce the right product. This emotional woman cannot be very operative by someone that's careless concerning their great emotional state. Whenever a machine needs a mechanical engineer to repair it, it has to have someone that truly knows what they're doing, and know what type of machine that needs to be diagnosis. Each machine(woman) has its own manufacturing instructions, and displays all the labels to operate this machine properly. The labels are her physical components with sensual gestures, instructions, and her behaviors. The operator(man) has to put these manufacturing components into actions with a very rational mind, and gestures with emotional contents. Failure to operate this machine with knowledge, wisdom, and understanding only will lead to a broken inoperative machine that has the capacity to produce greatly with the right operator. This machine runs on emotional fuel only. Which only means the way to communicate, is with emotional mannerism at times for there to be a great understanding for a future enduring relationship.

UNCONTROLLABLE EMOTIONS

Now we come to the topic of uncontrollable emotions. Control is one major thing that we all hate to lose, or for someone to utilize on us by any means. So what must we do to keep our emotions in check? We all know what can happen when emotions builds up with frustrations, stress, and being psychologically overwhelmed. Whenever these emotions becomes intensified, and the person that's driven by these emotions seeks no longer to talk, they just react with fury. Only because this emotional person has suppressed their feelings. This suppression will only build with great fury of vengeance to attack the perpetrator or potential perpetrator. There are many ways emotions can be acted out that's ferociously uncontrollable. Whenever a woman, and her partner have talked about something that tainted her feelings. This partner can't repeat the same hurtful action, but if he continues to disregard her feelings she will become bold in her acts to get this affair corrected. This emotional boldness leads to reactions with great audacity. These uncontrolled emotions will cause some women to jump in the bed with another man, only because her man has cheated on her numerous of times. At these times her feelings will scream with emotional intensity from within, "*I'm fed up with this shit!!* So she will prove to her partner that she can do it too, and do it better! So whenever her and her new male partner would have sexual encounters, she will do things to him she never has done in her entire life to a man. The thing she always founded despicable or nasty, she will do to please this new lover. These uncontrollable emotions forces her to act contrary to her own self morals. Uncontrollable emotions are very dangerous, and they can also be very productive to fix the problem with great intensity to never be repeated.

Some women have become alcoholics, dope addicts, lesbians, murders, and professional killers due their past experiences with the wrong man or men. Some women have become emotional challenges for men, due to the fact of not having a father figure. Usually when a woman has uncontrollable emotions, she will be emotionally forced into doing something very detrimental to herself. This only shows the great love she once had for a man, and vows to never love another man that hard or deeply again. Some women have landed themselves in prison houses due to uncontrollable emotions. This emotion has driven some women to kill, murder their mate, emotionally torment her mate, stalking, and perform acts of arson to her cheating partner's house or car. These uncontrollable actions has also cause many men to lose their jobs, due to some women calling his jobs using offensive language on the phone to whomever answers the phone. Once she has called and let it be known that she is the partner of this man, that works at this certain place of employment, she switches into overdrive with uncontrollable emotions to pay him back at all cost! Even if it means for him to lose his job.

Some women seek the child support agency, and forces the man to pay monies out of spite, which is uncontrollable emotions. I'm not saying that she shouldn't seek, and get was due to her for child-care. Only if she really needs that financial assistance, but some have done this just to get even emotionally. Which is right down evil! These uncontrollable emotions has also cause many women to become mentally insane for life. Only because they couldn't function no longer without the same man, or if the man was very abusive.

One of the main things we have to truly consider, when it come to emotions is the energy that's strong and very powerful within the human breast. This emotional energy is very unlimited, but limited through our kaleidoscopic vision. I'll discuss emotional power when we come to the chapter on emotions and success. If we don't control our emotions, this powerful energy called emotion will get away from us-destroy things that's very precious and valuable for our lives. All we should do and need to do is just stop for a moment, and consider what needs to be done intelligently. This powerful energy that God blessed us humans to have is very powerful and designed by His great wisdom. This only means that prudence, is how this energy called emotions is to be controlled and utilized. Emotion is like "a fish that takes to the water for survival," that same goes with energy and all living organism. Emotion was giving to the human as a fuel mechanism to build its life constructively by all means for its survival. So control your emotions, and don't let emotions control you.

Whenever there is domestic violence a surge of uncontrollable emotions are running rampant with fury! This rage and emotional vengeful tempers flares up with much retribution from the one that felt betrayed. Women have pulled, jerked, and hit their men without thinking, because they are driven by emotional rage that has caused many innocent men to be put in jail for domestic violence. Often times this does happen when man becomes tired of being his woman's punching bag, and when this happens she calls the police for assault. I'm not saying that a man should hit a woman by any means, but women tend to push the issue. Only because the so-called law will favor her because of her soft nature to be ruled by the state, verses man's strong nature to be conquered by the state called laws. She gets away with striking the man without him using any defensive methods. A woman can also physically hurt a man, just a well has man can hurt a woman physically. This needs to be seriously considered! There has been numerous of people severely hurt by domestic violence, due to uncontrollable emotions. Some women have used this domestic violence has a form of pay-back. Knowing that the police will believe her story over his, so she will have the man put in jail which is totally wrong, but this what happens when emotions are running wild and lose. Uncontrollable emotions are like a machine that runs ineffectively, and needs repairing fast, quick and effectively to operate optimally.

Emotional Anger

This topic I would approach from a fundamental standpoint; concerning words as we begin this subject on anger and emotion. The word we will use, is danger. This is a mechanism I've used with my kids and with a few adults. If we look at the word "*danger*," you will see the word "*anger*" in the midst. Do you think this is all a coincident? Me I figured some clever bastards sat down with some wise men, and brought this shit to fruition for those that's able to see the bedrock of words and their meanings. If you look at the word "*woman*," we see the word "*man*," and the same for "*women*." You see the word "*men*," no different than the word "*she*" we see "*he*," and "*her*" the same thing. Let's think about this for a moment. We as humans are all tied together no matter how many of us fail to see and recognize the wisdom. The great unity of words, animals, trees, and mainly the Human-Family per se' are a universal unity. So what drives us to be angry, and attack another person that is some else's love one. Whether daughter, son, uncle, aunt, grandparents, mother and father. Knowing we wouldn't like it, if some was projecting their anger on us. So, why do we do it to another person? Anger can be good also. To never let no one step on you, or use you without any consideration, and mainly the passion of anger that drives us to rise above mediocrity. Many people claim to be religious, and many claim we're all God's children. So why do we attack our brother or sister, when the wise Father-God sees this? Are we driven by emotions, or are we driven by intelligence? Emotions and intelligence suppose to work together to build, and create the life we deeply feel and desire to have. Not recognizing the wisdom of anger, and emotions will leads us to dangerous regretful actions. These actions has been the cause of many people's limited futures. Many have been mentally tormented, greatly discouraged, uncontrollable with misguided actions, resentful, and suppressed with anger. These feelings has the will power to build up within these walls of the human body. The human body is fashioned and designed with many cells. Then we wonder why the place jail is called a cell-block. No different than the jail-cell we put ourselves in, due to our emotional danger. Breaking the <u>Law of Self </u>we only incarcerate ourselves. Which only becomes an island of loneliness and depression. If humans were meant to be alone, none of us would be here. Adam would still be in his paradise lonely. Loneliness can lead to anger and self unworthiness. Knowing we can do better, but yet keep repeating the same old dead tactics.

Nowadays, they have therapist, psychologist, and counselors to treat people for anger management. If you can't control your own life, then someone will definitely control it for you! That's only because you lack the prudence to understand how emotions is to be used. Whenever you have to pay someone to tell you what you need to do concerning your own life is great stupidity! Like I've told many guys during an open session, while attending a book club that was diverse with men and women. Two guys opened with talks about having the skills of pimps and players was the way to deal with women. These guys were pushing the issues of wanting to emulate the skills of players. I've told these guys, "that lifestyle isn't for everybody, and take it from a woman that knows." These guys will have many problems trying to control one woman, and will go out to find another woman which will cause them even more problems. Only because they lack the skill of controlling themselves. Most men will do stupid shit, when they're angry at their woman. They will go out find another woman out of sheer anger and ignorance. These same men will find themselves divorced, paying child support, and encounter many other unseen things. These idiots will let their ego drive them emotionally angry, with limited understanding due to their chauvinistic male egoism. Women love to make men angry at times. If she knows without a sheer doubt, that she can make him angry without him going to far other than yelling. She will put him to the emotional test. This anger shows her the emotional content that she wanted to see, that indicates that he truly cares. Because no one will get angry, yell and fuss or even ride someone per se' to bring out the best, if they didn't give a damn! So emotions has the capacity to show women as well as men how much someone really cares. Also forcing someone to become emotionally angry, to see what's lurking beneath the normal thoughts, and feeling of that person can be good. This only triggers their emotions to reveal their true feelings. Whenever emotions are forced intentionally by someone with great prudence, that emotional power; without control will attack, and yell out some underline feelings that's been hidden concerning that person's true feelings about you and them. There has been times when we acted on our emotions and went too far. Then and only then, do we regret what we did out of anger. This act can never be taken back or forgotten. The same thing happens when we yell something offensive, and hurtful to someone we claim to love dearly. These words that we have yelled out from brute anger, if they're harsh and detrimental to the person, then we apologize for these words that can't change the fact of the matter. That person might accept our apology, but they will never forget what you said or did. We all know that we should think before we act, but we still foul up with this over, and over, and over again. Majority of people today are masters of fouling up. They are repeating the same thing many times. As the saying goes, "practice makes perfect". That only means we have perfect fools, shallow minds, and unchecked ignorance hoping for a difference. What can be more ludicrous that looking for a difference, but yet doing the same thing day in and night out. Many of us don't have the same mate we had fifteen or twenty years ago. This just goes to show that our minds are less powerful than our emotions. There's no wonder the present world is in a state of catastrophic flux, due to our limited intelligence. There are many present day psychologist that have made mention what our ancestors have said years ago in there writings, "that the future world of human-beings will only use 10% of their brains," and we see the results of this 10%. If you're truly intelligent as you say you are, look at your acts and the results of those acts. Do you see the kind of life you want or wish to live? If you don't see it, ask yourself why not? It's just an indication of your intelligence that's lacking, and your emotional anger is working without the power of thought. Without creative intellect and emotional power no one can spark the flame of true happiness. Many people today are trying to find happiness from drugs and alcohol, which only sets the stage of self destruction. Happiness is allusive. Many of us fail to understand that happiness is like power, it's always fleeing far in the distance from us, and we continue to pursue it. When the core of happiness evades us, then we become very disturbed within ourselves that forces us to become emotionally angry all over again. Unchecked anger is dangerous! You and I know this, so why am I repeating what we both assume to know, or do we?

EMOTIONAL DISTURBANCE

There are many things that's causing emotional disturbances for many us, whether men or women. The world presently is in a state of great flux with wars, lacking employment, doctors providing deadly medicines(side effects), cancer epidemics, kids and their behaviors whether at home or at school are running rampant, lacking of income, home invasions, business scams, technology with great exposure, political rhetoric and lies, and mainly the lack of respect for one another. All these things are effecting us emotionally that is disturbing our capacity to think rationally on a grand scale for life to be happily and endurable.

Other than these present life catastrophes that's causing men and women emotional disturbance; majority of women has experienced some horrific relationship in the past that's causing them emotional disturbance in their present adult years. Women that come from a past of being molested or raped by their father(step-fathers), brother(s), uncles, relatives or by a stranger, causes women to not trust men fully. This horrific past of rape and molestation leaves a deep scar on these women emotional state of being, that puts them in state of apprehension and emotional depression. Many of these adult women that have encounter these rapes, molestations, and child-abuse felt greatly neglected by their mothers or whomever the person they confided in concerning these abuses. These emotional disturbances have caused many women to become alcoholics, drug addicts, pill poppers, killers, murders, homeless and clinically depressed for life. There are many young girls and boys that are coming of age from an abusive past, which causes their adult life to have many great unhealthy challenges.

Another thing that causes many women to have emotional disturbance is not fulfilling their dreams. Their dreams of being married to "Mr. Good-bar or Mr. Right" or the man they're presently with. Many women that come from a good family back-ground tend to grow up with many hopes and dreams. These unfulfilled dreams for one reason or another puts a strain on women's emotional psychology. This forces women to become hopeless, because their dreams hasn't fruition and this can lead them to be emotional disturbed. This emotional disturbance can effect women to be totally un-submissive. Many successful women know how it feels to have a vision, and seek to fulfill that vision that appears to be long—overdue can be very emotionally draining, emotionally taxing, and mainly emotionally disturbing. Having plans that never works out can also be very disturbing to that person that always plan their future events. Whenever these plans backfire, fall short, or go contrary to their vision for happiness only then does the great fury of internal emotional disturbance resurfaces.

Having a relationship that started out with happiness, and later it seems to fall apart, or happiness appears to evade this relationship leads her to feel greatly emotional disturbed. This disturbance causes the women to question herself whether this relationship is falling apart because what she is doing, not doing or whether her physical appearance is the cause of this disturbed relationship. Many women fail to really know who they are before they engage into a relationship. This can lead to a breakdown with a great change as life continues to unfold. We all change mentally and physically has we get older. These changes play a major role on our psychic that's very emotional disturbing to grow old. Women that get minimum attention from their lover or mate feels emotional neglected, which in essence cause her to feel emotionally disturbed. This disturbance will cause her to question her mate. Usually she will ask, "is there another woman that's getting his attention?" Sometimes there isn't another woman, but because the man is mentally occupied with some endeavor and she feels neglected; she will approach this from that stand point because of her emotional disturbance. This emotional disturbance is also a form of emotional blindness. The blindness is the lack of seeing what's really going on, but since her love is deep for her mate she only see through the lens of love, which is emotional.

Why did God create women to be emotional beings, and men to be logical beings? There has to be some great wisdom behind this great creative organized format for men and women. If we read in the Book of Genesis we come to acknowledge women has to labor or work from her body, which is close to the heart, and man had to work or labor from his head (the brow). So this wise format makes women creatively emotional or physical, and man to be logical which is mental. Why are we having so much problems or lacking understanding of ourselves? Yet we tend to push our religious belief on others about something we believe to be true and can't see the fact ourselves. God has never been seen by the physical eye, because people can't feel the god within themselves to see it in other people, is why God has not been seen by the majority. If we truly recognize this Oneness and implement this awareness on a day to day bases we would truly see a better world. To see our lover or the one we choose to be with daily, and fail to work together for the betterment of our lives is a daily tragedy. Logic(man) and emotion(woman) must work together. Two halves that comes together will eventual make a complete whole.

Emotional Success

There's many ways to become successful, whether by investing in real estate, stocks, or franchisees just to name a few. The lack of having money, and today's financial crisis is causing many of us to be very emotional, whether financial or psychology insecure. To become emotionally successful is work within itself. This success has to deal with the inner being of the person. Every millionaire had to control his or her emotions, but used their emotions as a fuel and passion mechanism to carry them through temporary defeats, to continue until their goal or goals has been achieved. If every millionaire didn't control his or her emotions before they became millionaires, they would have never became millionaires because of the recklessness of uncontrollable emotions. Success is a personal calling from within, and this calling is that inner emotional calling. This calling fuels the person to do something, that's drive the person to reach a certain plateau of excellence whether international, local or personal.

Growing up in a state poverty can be very emotional to become successful. Poverty for some is a very motivational tool to become somebody to remove life's hardships. Seeing your love—ones or yourself living in a horrific life on day to day bases of degradation and havoc can fuel you or many to become emotionally successful. Always lacking the fortunate things that others tend to always have place some of us in a emotional disturbance of embarrassment. So the lifestyle of struggling economically on a continuous bases, tends to fuel that emotionally deprived person to do something, to remove one-self from this life of unhappiness and stress. This is when emotion is very healthy and good, that it drives a person to be become successful.

Emotional success is also having the right person we've always dreamed to have for a husband, wife, boyfriend, or girlfriend as long this type of person is in or part our lives. Having emotional success enhances us to feel like we're on top of the world. So in a since, success is not always measured in numbers of monetary things, but in the number of years you and the right person has shared, and not wasting a minute in this short existence called life. Even though by today's standard success is measured by the monetary things, cars, homes, and clothes and educational degrees. Many people today have all these things, and we hear about these people committing suicide, marrying the wrong spouse, going economically broke from being emotional hyped, and later becoming clinically depressed. We also have read about millionaires going broke after being taken by a prostitute or a con-man. Many of us would think or say, "how could a millionaire be involved with a low-life despicable person, he or she has to be crazy?" Some millionaires are the loneliest people on the planet earth because they can't trust people. They believe people only want them for their money. So their lives becomes a life in a shell to prevent themselves from being a victim of being used for their money.

You can become the next millionaire or have the best relationship only if you know how to control your emotions. You cannot get carried too far away from the mark of sanity, that makes it too difficult to get back to a normal state of being. So I conclude, that success is yours, only if know how to use the fuel of emotion to become successful. Many of us have heard the saying or cliché', "that money can't and will no buy you happiness, or when you die you can't take it with you, so you better enjoy life and money now while you have it!" These are the words of emotional mediocre minds that are hinder by their self fears. I'm not saying that fear isn't good within some form or fashion. Because there are some things in this life to fear, if you really have a desire to become successful. The moment you become successful within yourself, you will know it, and your emotions will be on a high of euphoria of self elation.

Every woman hates to be classified or grouped with other women. We all feel as though we as women are all different from the rest, and especially different from the last woman that her present husband or boyfriend had. We as women are all different in our scope of vision, our personality mainly, and very different in our characteristics as women. You must agree with this totally, but most men feel as though all women are the same. For example, if her last relationship was with a man that didn't have a drive to reach another level economically or intimately, and she was ok with that for years, and this relationship breaks-off which effect her emotionally with hurt, pain and guilt as usual. Then she meets another man that's very different from her last relationship, and if this relationship is with a man that's driven to climb the economical ladder, and he also displays charm intimately that makes her feel special, this can be a great battle because of her emotional warped view to change for greatness financially and emotionally. Women today fail to change due their past pains, which has force many of them to protect themselves emotionally. The best for her can be right under her nose and right before eyes. She fails to see what type of man she can have for life due to her emotional neglect and insight, which is presently detrimental. This will spoil her one in a life-time chance to be with an emotional-financial champion. We all have to make changes to advance in this life, or be left in the dust of times. Changes are definitely inevitable, and no matter how we hate changes they will happen! If we look at the changes in the seasons, we can see the wisdom and power of changes. Changes affect everyone domestic or foreign. When winter is here, we no longer wear our summer clothing, and when summer is here we no longer wear our winter clothing. This just goes to show us how, and why changes are powerful and necessary.

WOMEN, MEN AND EMOTIONS

Women and men are having a great relational breakdown, that divides them, and that breakdown is called emotion and ego. Women that are driven by emotion without logic becomes a nagger to men, and men turn a deaf ear to what she's talking about. Only because this emotional driven woman seems to be dramatic as we say today. Her dramatic emotions sounds illogical to the man, so he ignores her, and do not wish to hear what she has to say. Women and men are both emotional beings. Women's emotions are strictly physiological with great feelings, and men's emotions are driven by egoism which is strictly psychological. This mental and physical emotional breakdown creates a great divide, and the lack of trust between two sexes that's created to attract and not repel. Since men and women are having a great divide, and lacking the trust that's needed to fulfill natures awesome cycle; it's causing men to be with men and women to be with women. This just goes back to what are ancestors have said about us future humans only using 10% of our brains. Many of us has spend 5 to 10 years or 15 to 20 years of our short lives with someone we don't want, can't do good with, will not do better for, and only come to find out who we are or seem to be through the years of relational set-backs and upsets. These are the same people that says, "life is short," but look at all this time that's been utilize to find ourselves, and the right person for life.

Women have been blessed to know firsthand by nature's great plan, that we all have to go through something to achieve something worth having. Women that have children or a child had to bear a child in painful labor only to see that great life or seed of love. She had to sacrifice her life to bare her child or children, which some women have died giving birth. So in order for men to be here, women had to bare boys through labor, which is "pain for the great life of gain".

Here's an episode that is happening concerning an emotionally beautiful woman that was broken hearted, due to her husband's infidelity, and verbal abuse. She told me, that her husband of 15 years lies began to surface, and he had the nerve to tell her she can have a boyfriend if she wants to because he didn't give a damn! I told her that was all bullshit, and not to believe what he says. He is seeking justification to do what he always wanted to do, because unwise husbands feel tied down and caged up. It makes him feel bonded to you, and not to his sexual ego, which effects majority of men today. So, she asked, 'What makes a man say he doesn't care about his wife, or say harsh things like this? I don't understand! I have given this man 15 years of my life, and this is what he do and does to me. I don't understand!!!' I asked, "Do you what your man back, and to also teach him a lesson?" She told me she did, so I give her some simple instructions on what to do, whether to make it or break it, because his ego is what we're going to turn and shake inside of him deeply. I told her to type a letter with romantic words of poetry, to go to the store and buy some cologne, a long white T-shirt that's for a man basically, also buy a smooth jazz CD, and when he comes home from one of his business trips, then go to the nearest post-office, and mail the package. Also use any ole' return addresses with a male's name to get his ego and emotions running with rampant anxiety, and be prepared for the show down of male egoism, that's all hype and bullshit when it comes to another man taking his spot. She informed me when the package came through the mail that this man had a damn fit, and that he was raising some much sand, that for days he kicked and made one hell of a fuss. I told her to tell him one thing, and that will put things in prospective for you mainly, and give him something to considered greatly. I told her to say these few words, and watch his reactions and comments. She told him, 'what's the problem with me having another man, you said you didn't care, if you don't care why are you getting angry?' She said he stood there looking dumb founded, and he has became a better husband, and at times he always bring up the invisible man that exist in his mind, but doesn't exist at all. Most men try like hell to make a woman submit to his will, power, and control. When she submits, what usually happens? He loses this control that he demanded

26

through abuse, lies, betrayal, and ignorance. If men play their part like Father-Time, which works in unisons with Mother-Nature, they will produce and fruition a life of success and a healthy relationship. We are all surrounded by Great Wisdom that only a few, whether men or women can conceive these Universal signs for living harmoniously with self and others.

So what is it going to take for women and men to get this great universal plan together? Women have to understand that men are logical and rational. Men have to understand that women are emotional physical heartfelt beings. Failing to understand the nature of each other's gender and make-up will forever be a relational havoc. Without this understanding between both sexes, we are forever headed to a universal destruction. Even the animals know that opposite sexual genders is the only way to produce, and remain in equilibrium.

I sincerely feel for women of today and their caged emotions that's like a emotional rollercoaster. What I mean about caged up emotions, is that she hopes and hopes her man will change his emotionally abusive ways. The abusive ways of her man is all up to her and her emotional tactics.

EMOTIONAL DANGERS

What can be dangerous about emotions? Many my say, "uncontrollable emotions, lashing-out emotional with fury, acting-out, and been depressed." I've made mention of the danger of emotions. Uncontrolled emotions or feeling are dangerous, but one thing that makes emotions dangerous, is what we do with this passion of life force or energy. Many times women may say something while the kids around, because she's angry, and the kids wind up repeating what they have heard their mother say unconsciously due to anger and stress. The kids will repeat these words not knowing what these words truly mean, only because mother has said these words. Now the kids thinks that it's ok to say these ugly words. Kids will grow up thinking it's ok to use these words, and not knowing when to use the right words makes it dangerous for the kids and adults. Many adults have gotten fired from their jobs of being mentally and verbally overwhelmed, and lacking to control their tongues in front of customers or becoming very aggressive with other employees with harsh offensive words.

Uncontrollable sexual gratification can be very dangerous, especially on jobs. Women and men have taken their personal lives to work, and this has cause many to have unwanted relationships. These relationships always starts out good, exciting, and very pleasurable. Having a relationship with an fellow employee becomes dangerous when both employees passions and desires becomes great. Their sexual experiences forces them sometimes to sneak off and have a short sexual rendezvous. After having many of these sexual quick rendezvous will continue to grow without the rational thing to do, which is wait for the appropriate time for these sexual rendezvous. These sexual rendezvous will keep happening a few times to see if they can get away with it numerous of times, will only increase their desire to do this over and over again to one day get caught. Only emotion was driving these two individuals to continue their sexual desire without regards or respecting their place of business. Not only just having sexual episodes at work is dangerous, but being greatly driven by their sexual emotions they will have sexual episode without protection knowing they both have other sexual partners at home. Emotions that come to work with this person or persons, can cause many to have infected the other with a social deadly disease or an unexpected child is a real serious priority.

We all know how drugs and alcohol are very dangerous when they become addictive, and many of us will use these dangerous elements for a crutch. Women that feel useless, abused, and neglected sometime will turn to pills, alcohol, and some drug to lift them up when they feel greatly depressed. Because these women are angry of their cheating husbands or boyfriends that continue to be disloyal or dishonest with their relationship, and she loves him too much to leave, so she will turn to alcohol or drugs to cope. This danger is emotionally unhealthy for her to function normally. Not only will this force one to become a druggy, but now the family no longer trust this emotional alcoholic or drug abuser. Not only is this emotional disturbed woman a drug user, an alcoholic, but also an environmental risk for the social environment of her love ones and others in society as whole.

Another emotional danger is shopping without the rational mind to be frugal or logical between wants and needs. Many women have driven their spouse or boyfriends to become angry, and break off the present relationship; to due to the women's lack of been frugal or rational when it comes to shopping or spending money. Emotional shopping is a very, very and extremely emotional habit. This cause the women to consume, consume, and consume many things that's not needed! A lot of women have went into financial debt because of uncontrollable emotional spending. Their emotions are driving them to spend, and also these women will defend their reason for spending money uncontrollably. This is due to unchecked emotions that are running rampant for a quick delusional euphoria.

Acting-out on these emotions is the real danger. These acts that has been committed without the least regard for the other person and self, has a great possibility to be dangerous with unwanted retribution.

WOMAN THAT
EMOTIONAL MACHINE

I will give several examples, on ways, reasons how, and why women can be similar to a machine. I have also made mention that this great feminine machine is powerful when utilized properly. The core and make-up of women needs a certain type of fuel to operate and stimulates their inner beings. Their inner being is their personality, not their characteristic which is different in magnitude and scope. See the personality of every person whether woman, man, boy or girl is who they really are. The character of each individual is different. The character of each person forces us to wear a different mask at certain times and places. Also our characteristics forces us to wear a different mask due to the emotional situations. The mask that we all wear at different times, forces us to be someone other than who we truly are to protect ourselves from hurt, pain, or the thought of being stupid for one reason or another. This feminine machine that the world of men truly needs majority of the times, has caused the uncontrolled ego of men to take this great female machine for granted. Majority of men looks at this feminine machine as just a sexual object without feelings. This causes much stressors of insecurity that men fail to understand. Knowing damn well that this machine is framed, fashioned, and created by the Hands of Wisdom. These Hands of Wisdom saw fit for women to function strictly on emotional understanding and for men to function totally on logical wisdom. Some men are still boys due to their lacking of a male role model, lacking of wisdom to be honest and letting their egos rule. Men that use women for their sexual gratification only fail to understand the wisdom that comes with women and society. Women are the producers of society. Without women there wouldn't be a society! Even though I use a machine synonymously to emphasis a point pertaining to women,

it doesn't mean that I look down on my sister women, because I don't!!!
I am a woman, a lady, a Queen! (In fact I love being around my loyal
women sisters, and I also love doing business with them.)

Majority of women had to go through men like grades of fuel to find the
right grade of emotional fuel for their life to be emotionally productive.
Majority of young-women in their early lives had to experience several
different types of fuel(young boy). Diesel fuel stinks, and it also burns
slowly. Usually the first experience of life for young-women and young-
men stinks like diesel. Young-women move slowly like stinky slow
burning diesel. Only because they are afraid and inexperienced about
sex in order to fulfill these young-men sexual desires. Not only does
diesel burns slow it is made only for certain types of machines and
vehicles. When these same young women become older and their
physical adolescent—hormonal light comes on, it forces some of them
to try regular fuel(teenage boy), but since it was like other fuel(sexual
driven boy) just regular, and only for those that are cheap and useless she
moves on to another type of fuel and grade. Only because the diesel was
young, naively dumb, and driven by his sexual organ. Next, she tries
the plus fuel(young man), which seems to work good over time, but the
person couldn't keep up the optimal work that's needed for her machine
to work at an optimal standard for a long productive life. Finally, she
tries the best grade of fuel that is supreme(a wise man), but only by going
through so many emotional hurtful experiences. She becomes mature,
and the stage is set for her to be truly honest and sincere with herself.
By these life emotional experiences she finds the proper fuel(wise man)
for her emotional machine to produce a healthy loving relationship.

We have touched on sex concerning emotions elsewhere, but I will
make mention of sex and emotions from another stand point. The
example, I will give is when the woman's boyfriend or husband has
taken her emotional love for granted. That's usually when men become
bored, and seek excitement and adventure elsewhere. Only when he gets
caught, and she fills hurt, vulnerable, and seeks emotional vengeance,
sex becomes the pay-back tool. This emotional pain will cause her to
seek some other man to understand her that makes her feel wanted,
needed, important, and beautiful. Whenever this affair becomes sexual
she will woo him, please him totally, and sex him down almost till the

death of him or her. *("In other words excuse my French, she will fuck him like she never has fucked her husband, boyfriend or any other man before in her life.")* Most men fail to understand that any woman that has been hurt by her initial lover after many years might really like you, but she has to satisfy her emotional painful psychology first and foremost! Which in essence she feels as though she has to pay her husband or boyfriend back for him having a sexual or any type of relationship with another woman or women, and breaking the loyalty, and dedication she has given to him for many years.

This machine has the power to produce greatly on a massive scale with the right partner that gives her the right fuel emotionally to operate. No machine can operate without some type of fuel or energy mechanism. Fortunately, women's types of fuel is emotion. So, what can men do or be without this great machine. Many men are fooling themselves thinking they don't need women, but yet many of them are acting like women. Which only goes to show the world of their ignorance. Trying to be something they are not, no matter how many operations performed on the core of man's anatomy is a man, and the core of a woman is a woman no matter how many operations that has been performed on her to be like a man. You can not remove the DNA of your gender! These people are emotionally and psychologically fucked up for life. If any machine was made to be a car, no matter how many changes made to that car it is still is a car. No human can alter what God has created. Whether doctor or a scientific genius as we called them has the wisdom to overcome the Creator's universal wisdom. The Great wisdom has created all things we need in order to survive, and see the signs of reality called the "<u>is</u>" and not be ignorantly driven by blindness called the "<u>ought</u>." There is many things we don't understand in this creation, and many of us fail to understand who we are, and we are one with ourselves daily, and still fail to know who we are. God does not make mistakes, only frail weak emotional disturbed minded humans make costly deadly mistakes.

When it comes to this machine called woman, most men fail to understand what it takes to keep this machine in a state of emotional optimal euphoria and happiness. Women desire and lone to have a man that knows how to operate her sexual emotional machine with knowledge that gives her the greatest pleasure that she ever imagined a woman could ever have experienced. Men today have tried many things to please a woman sexually, mentally, financially and emotionally. Many of these men continue to fail at this endeavor, because of their egos which prevent them from knowing what women desires most. All relationships begins well, and in due time this intellectual mannerism that's appealing with respect, and the need to make a "first impression" as we say sooner or later fails. When his first impression of respect and charming acts starts to dissipate and becomes banal, then comes the emotional strife and egoism that breaks down this great possibility for a wonderful relationship to endure the test of time, which is real love.

Whenever this fire of desire starts to die, it is an indication she is looking elsewhere if she is not emotionally weak and foolish to remain in a love drought. So men must understand what it takes to keep his woman on her toes like a ballet dancer. She will forever be down with you like, "roots to a tree, and like a car with four flat tires with three spare!" 'Ha, Ha!!

Men have to learn and find a way to understand these emotional machines, and women have to find a way to understand men with big egos. Lacking the understanding that's greatly needed will be an ongoing problem for both sexes. Men today are becoming greatly in love with their cars, trucks, motorcycles, video games, jewelry and their computers with nude clips except the machine that can reward them with great love that's greatly gratifying. I've heard many dope-heads, alcoholics, and pill poppers say that, "getting high is better that sex." My only comment is that nothing can be greater than sex or making love to the right person. Drugs kills the mind and its power to see reality. Drugs and alcohol are nothing but emotional driven stimulators. Anything that destroys the mind, will cause anyone to speak or make stupid comments. Any man that turns a woman on to drugs, alcohol, popping pills has to be greatly stupefied. "Why would any woman do anything that's destructively emotional to her well being?" Women feels, and drugs gives her a scenes of feelings that's deadly, but due to her emotional physiological core she becomes addicted to these deadly feelings. This deadly feeling will destroy this great wise machine to breakdown little by little, and she will no longer be a help or productive for herself, her kids, and the society. She becomes a ragged useless machine that sits and rusts with emotional corrosion. This emotional machine has to be very careful about things that makes her feel good. This feeling of goodness can be an allusion. Just because it felt good does not mean it really is good. If any man that was selfishly good to any woman, and she displays the goodness of elation for him, it later will become a emotional sadness. Most men seek to have this control or power over women. He can't have power over women when he loves to have sexual relations with her only. As long as men has this need to have sexual relation excessively it drives him to cheat, pay for it, go to strip clubs, and watch internet x-rated flicks, who will for—ever be emotional powerless. Men that feel powerless usually become abusive to women. Women that are abused by their mate will be emotionally dangerous, emotionally angry, emotionally disturbed, emotionally fearful, emotionally insecure, and her emotional success will forever be a great endeavor to achieve within her and for herself, to be that great Emotional Machine called Woman.

Learning what makes a woman tick and tock, is by far one of the hardest thing that men must aspire to know is a must! It is one of the most driven goals and achievements that some have attempted only to come up disappointed! The lack of truly understanding the nature of women will forever be a flux for all men's future relationships. This machine will give the informational print out concerning her feelings and things that she hates from her past that she emotionally dreads to repeat. But only a few men truly knows how to listen. Women's emotional contents comes with many forms depending on her outlook on life.

My delightful intelligent, strong minded and wonderful man gives me a great sense of love, respect and responsibility to endure with him for our future. I have the oil that lubricates his head, he has the super gasoline that fuels my heart of excitement that's mixed with exotic drama. Finally, I have the right fuel(man) and wisdom to push my right buttons that will put my machine in optimal emotional work, which is compatible with his operative skills for us to work productively.

This book is for all women no matter your ethnicity, race, religion, and nationality. You are that great feminine machine that is greatly needed!

I'm the first to say that your fashion, frame, and design to bring societal elation, sexual happiness, and being the great producers for the family and the world as a whole is very important. Whether men realize this or not, you should from your emotional experiences has a woman, love yourself first and foremost! Respect, love, and peace to you all women around the world.

Sincerely,
Delady

LOVE

Love where have you been all my life,
I try like hell to be right,
But all you do is evade my heart,
I give my love and you rip me apart,
I try again and again,
I still attract the same ugly inconsiderate man,
I give you my time and energy,
And all you do is abuse me,
I give my heart and kisses,
But you just beat and kick me,
I open my legs to show you my feelings,
All you do is roll over my sincerity,
I drink and smoke,
But your love treats me like a joke,
I yearn for your love and hugs,
All we do is fight and fuss,
I pray for the right man to come along,
But all I get is the same ole' egoistical clone,
I give and give and give and give,
The treatment makes it harder to live,
I will not commit emotional suicide,
Love I'm dieing inside,
Yet my heart is open wide,
I search and plead for love to rescue or save me,
Now I've found my love deep within me,
Love is here to stay with me for Eternity.

HUGS AND KISSES

I loved the way he kisses and hugs me,
He makes me feels important and protected sincerely,
His hugs are masculine and I feel secure,
His kisses are like the doctors' healing cure,
What a man to make my heart race with passion,
He gives me time and attention without me asking,
He kisses me before he leaves for work,
I feel for those women that live with them jerks,
When he comes back home from work,
He kisses and hugs me with a joy that I elatedly smirk,
I pray that God bless us to stay together forever,
He makes me feel important, beautiful, and clever,
I love it when he hugs me when we're in bed,
He whispers sweet words as we lay head to head,
When he says, "Baby I love You" it's so wonderful,
His hugs and kisses are like a thunder,
My life with him is very electric,
I know is he heavenly sent, because he's exotically angelic

Emotional Confusion

He kisses me passionately one day,
The next day he pushes me away,
He makes love to me exotically one night,
The next night he's out late and out of my sight,
He takes me to the finest restaurants,
Next I'm begging and pleading about what I want,
He calls me on the phone while I'm at home,
Then I don't hear from him and I'm all alone,
He always pays my beauty salon bills,
Then he complains that's economically unreal,
He treats me sweet in front of his friends,
When we depart from them it all ends,
He takes me to the finest boutiques,
Then he bitches he shouldn't bought them for me,
How much more can I take?
I love him too much to throw it all away,
What should I do?
Help because I'm emotionally confused.

EXOTIC LOVERS

He prepares a warm bath with rose petals for us,
Then he brings the wine with kisses and hugs,
We both make our way to the bedroom,
He puts on some smooth jazz that fills the room,
He kisses me passionately with strong hugs,
We lay in the bed, "ha, ha" exotic foreplay it feels like a drug,
He kisses me on my neck,
He licks me on the ear next,
He runs his hands and tongue over my breast,
He kisses my stomach and then my inner thigh,
He's very seductively smooth that I moan and sigh,
Then he tastes my nipples again,
Damn what a man,
He moves with rhythm and charm,
Damn his sex is the bomb,
Next he plays with my clitoris gentle and sweetly,
He drives me wild the way he touches me,
My juices gets to flowing that I'm very wet,
I'm begging and pleading for that joyous sex,
He enters my love tunnel with ease,
I sigh and moan for him to "fuck me",
He takes his time with smooth sexual grinds,
Soon we're in heaven making love eternally,
I sigh and moan even more and more exotically,
My vagina feels so good wrapped around his rod,
He strokes me and I scream calling, "God, ha, oh God,
After we reach our peak we drift off to sleep.

QUESTIONNAIRE

I will pose a question to all women to ponder this question deeply. Be truly honest with yourself or suffer the consequence!

Is the man you are presently with your partner, lover, husband or your sexual gravitational tool only?

Here's a question for the men.

How was King Solomon able to handle or deal with 700 hundred women (wives)? Think about that men! Because some of you men have extreme problems with your one woman, but will go out and create an outside or extra relationship with another woman.

Conclusion

We all have a lot to learn in this upside down world that's presently presenting many facets of trials and demanding endeavors. Economics is driving women and men to be emotional in some form and fashion. Today women and men are faced with many emotional encounters of sadness and madness. This emotional darkness is causing many of us to give little thought to our present issues, and react without thinking of the consequences that are very costly. Marriages and relationships are not lasting like the days of our grandparents, due to many catastrophic environmental and personal changes. Kids are lost because of the parents' issues of emotional stresses and emotional blindness. Parents are stressing and blaming the politicians for playing political games of power. Something has to be done about this topsy-turvy world of chaos! Only a few of us know that order comes out of chaos, but times has shown us that we have gone too far to turn back the stages of destruction! Or can we? It's so sad that we all claim and say we love our children dearly, but look at this present world that us adults has created for them to clean up is sadness versus madness. How can we put a heavy burden on our love-ones when many of us do not want some else's burden dumped on us. But yet we're doing the same thing to the kids of the future. If the head is sick mentally, then the body well display this same sickness, and if the body is sick, then the mind well think negative-sick thoughts. Since the politicians are the head that is setting the stage and rules that govern this societal body, it is leading us to live in a sick world that's vomiting all of societies' violent emotional impurities. The world is suffering from the lack of understanding one another and self. Many people in society claim not to be prejudice or racist, but we see that this comment on race is easier to say, than to put these words truly into actions for the betterment of the world. Women have been mistreated, because of man's ego fueling them to look at women as sexual machines, house maids, and mother's to always tend to the kids and nothing more. This has caused women to stand for a great reason and cause, which is called "Women's Lib," but this has gone too far also. Women are dating women and trying like hell to implement or act like men that they oppose. This is sick! It also goes against the Law of nature. The eyes can only see what the mind's eye chooses to see. Too much emotion has and will drive any woman to hell! Women are and is somebody! No less or no greater than men. We all have a part to play that is important to one another in this <u>One</u> diverse human society.

One of my business associate stated this when I told him I was writing a book about women, men and emotions, "Women need to learn how to control their emotions, and men need to learn how to deal with these emotions."

Recommended Books
for Reading

PLAYA-ISM
Are you a player? Or are you being played?

Psychological Skullduggery
"In a world of manipulation, deceit and ruthlessness is
of the norm and all is fair play."

Political Veil: Positioning For Power

· ·

(New Spellbound Book on Short Stories/Novel)

That Bitch Called Life

www.ingramcontent.com/pod-product-compliance
Lightning Source LLC
Chambersburg PA
CBHW030540290526
45786CB00004B/1796